# *Fractal Song* POEMS

Jerry W. Ward, Jr.

T0159398

BLACK
WIDOW
PRESS

Boston, MA

# Fractal Song   POEMS

Joseph S. Phillips and Susan J. Wood, Ph.D., Publishers
www.blackwidowpress.com

Design & production: Kerrie Kemperman

*Cover Image: Mandelbrot fractal by KH627, Creative Commons Attribution–ShareAlike 3.0 Unported license.*

ISBN-13: 978-0-9971725-2-2

Printed in the United States
10 9 8 7 6 5 4 3 2 1

## ACKNOWLEDGEMENTS

Some of these poems first appeared in *Iowa Review, Drumvoices Revue, Nimrod, The Black Scholar, Blind Alleys, OBSIDIAN, The Georgia Review, Black American Literature Forum, New Laurel Review, The Jabberwock,* and *Black Magnolias*. A few were published in *Mississippi Writers: An Anthology* (1988), *The Jazz Poetry Anthology* (1991), *Erotique Noire/Black Erotica* (1992), *Modern American Poets* (1994), *Catch the Fire!!!* (1998), *Sons of Lovers: Anthology of Poetry by Black Men* (2000) and *Black Gold: An Anthology of Black Poetry* (2014). I am grateful to the editors of these publications for their generous acts of faith.

—Jerry W. Ward, Jr.

## To Those Who Grieve the Death of a Poet

If you dream you are a star
More than a grain of dirt
Declare your poems to be
More than teaspoons of water
Dropped into a raving sea
You are more a fool
Than language has named you.
You worry death to death.
Your encrypted bones
Can, should you let them,
Lead you to bless the body
With the balm of love.

Recall. Spirit speaks
Echoes in the canyons of mind:
*Struggle. Nothing has ended*
*Change. Struggle. No peace arrived.*
*Struggle until the end. The end*
*Qualifies you with death*
*To mourn and bury the dead.*

# TABLE OF CONTENTS

**STARTS**
Complete incompletes
Imperatives conspire

Your Voice ~ 15
Open ~ 16
The Impossible All These Years ~ 18
Black Boy ~ 19
Trueblood ~ 20
Mississippi John ~ 21
Don't Be Fourteen ~ 22
Moods in South Sharp ~ 24
Son to Father ~ 26
On the Border of Constant Disaster ~ 28
Kafka ~ 29
Jazz to Jackson to John ~ 30

## MIDDLES
### Complete incompletes
### Imperatives conspire

Opening Night ~ 37

Serious ~ 39

Kwansaba 61907 ~ 41

Moment #1 ~ 42

A Modest Plea ~ 43

An April Observation ~ 44

A Peapicking Prayer ~ 45

Transition ~ 47

The Body Politic ~ 48

Salvation ~ 49

4 & 5 ~ 51

Love in a Foreign House ~ 55

Poems of Guilt and Innocence ~ 56

Fragility ~ 57

Blood and Black Fires ~ 58

Pregnant Memories ~ 61

That Day the Rainbow Died ~ 66

## ENDS
### Complete incompletes
### Imperatives conspire

Trayvon ~ 71
He Has Wonderful Eyes ~ 73
Poem 69 ~ 75
Winter Solitude ~ 76
Reparations ~ 78
Uncle Sam and Uncle Tom ~ 80
Footnote 666 ~ 81


"Postscript" by Kalamu ya Salaam ~ 83


Fusion ~ 89

# STARTS

Complete incompletes

Imperatives conspires

## YOUR VOICE

It's a magic thing
Sun and rain and poetry
Flooding in my memory,
But all I can remember
Is how you got over
A deep river
With amazing grace
And cured your blues
With natural rhythms.

## OPEN

*(for Alice Walker)*

You are open.
The delicate tracery
of your soul
is exposed.

You live a year's December.
The cold eyes cast
upon the patterns
of your being
are not often kind,
not always clean.

Within the heart
of the heart
of your being
is a strong castiron stove,
an eternal demon flame.
How otherwise explain
your warm survival?

Sometimes
I watch you,
time your exquisite poise.
Then you are
Zora or Marie Laveau

or a mystery
I do not presume
to understand.

At those times
I fear you most,
because I can
love you
for what you are.

## THE IMPOSSIBLE ALL THESE YEARS

Sometime before you hit forty,
You must step outside your bones,
Audit the maze your flesh has made.
And be amazed how much consequence
Morality has planted on your feet,
How much ambivalence is the harvest
Of your legs, how much lost potential
Is barned in your gut, how much
Opportunity has leaked from your pores.

From the outside, the prospect is not pretty;
Your living is like linen full of catfaces,
Your presence is a penitentiary riot.
You are criminal, a critical case
Of becoming the unregenerate image
Of yourself; but finding peace in your planet
You stride back inside to praise
The impossible all these years.

## BLACK BOY

Some black boys go deep south,
Chiseling attitudes,
Rise to recognition
Up north, somewhere
Somewhere up north
The compass cannot read.

Some black boys stay deep south,
Battling the cobwebs
Of a long and lonely dream,
Making something somewhere
Somehow out of nothing.

And then,
Some black boys
Know deep south
And only be.

## TRUEBLOOD

trueblood, he never heard
of incest and such mess
and worried only about pests
in his cotton crop,
looked on chaos and survived

trueblood, he always understood
what professors thought they could
he dipped snuff, drank rotgut stuff
and bought what labor bought,
looked on chaos and survived

trueblood, he never owned
a tailored suit, high-stepped
in cast-offs when he got'em,
was the holiest deacon in the church,
looked on chaos and survived

in all his ninety years
trueblood, he never uttered
the blind words "I've arrived,"
cause he stayed at home,
looked on chaos and survived.

## MISSISSIPPI JOHN: Southern Comfort Toast

Mississippi John knew Lena Horne
And all the greats of old,
But he clipped so straight
You would have sworn
He was a dap mack on the stroll.

Mississippi John was always seen
In a spanking new machine.
His Arrow shirts were white on white on white,
His vines were sharp as laser light.

He loved to boast, in signifying toasts,
Of conquests from coast to coast.
He'd been to Paris, Moscow, Timbuktu,
Done everything a blood can do,
And still looked young enough
To pass for forty-two.

Mississippi John must have had
The hoodoo that makes a young girl glad,
A magnet stone, a bag of lucky bones,
Cause his Johnson never lied about his Jones.

## DON'T BE FOURTEEN (in Mississippi)

Don't be fourteen
black and male in Mississippi
       they put your mind
       in a paper sack, dip it
       in liquid nitrogen
       for later consumption
Don't be fourteen
black and male in Mississippi,
have two 20/20 eyes,
feet that fail to buck, wing and tap,
a mouth that whistles
       they castrate you, wrap
       you in cotton-bailing wire
       while your blood still feels,
       feed you to the Tallahatchie
       as guilt-offering to blue-eyed susans

Don't be fourteen
black and male in Mississippi
       they say you a bad nigger
       named Bubba, a disgrace
       to the race in your first offense,
       and give you to Parchman
       for forty-eight years.
       You need, they say, a change to grow.

Don't be fourteen
black and male in Mississippi
        they say you a man at two.
        be one.
        when white boys ask
        why don't you like them,
        spit on them
        with your mouth closed.

## MOODS IN SOUTH SHARP

*Greenville, MS / April 27, 1934*

i am one
of the persons
of families that is
in very bad need
of aid
and up to this date
have been denied

so it have retch
the stage
that something
must be did


*Charleston, SC, 1993*

The waiter said

in those days
blind tigers roamed freely
in the streets and spoke in tongues
in those days
trickster winds

ripped off the roofs
to spite the bold ones
who drank their words
in speakeasy rebellion


*Atlanta in August, 1994*

if this morning looks
like a poem, like a symphonic fog
descending to compensate
a visual challenge,
or like the underwear of reality,

if this morning
burns your psychological feet,
moves Africans rapidly through Atlanta,
makes you sing you damn sure do not want to do
wrong
check your options.

## SON TO FATHER, WITH LOVE / GRAVESIDE PRAYER

You gave me jazzspace, Dad, a tempo for life,
but you never gave me love, and you only know
why I am. A gumbo gene-pool, Dad, you gave me
your brilliant frustration, cynical smile, your guts
and guile, the smarts to be no fool, but you never
   gave me love


dad, you gave me a real hard time,
an icebox of disappointments, nerves
pliant as jello, anger like a poison in my lungs,
hunger for approval, words to scar my heart.
But you never gave me love, nor asked
if I needed it to heal the burns of conscience.
And I don't know why I am as like you as I am.


You gave me an electric train when I was five.
I rode its tracks across a geography of my making,
a far distance where you became a bag of groceries,
a bottle of gin, a radio listening to a ballgame,
a crossword puzzle who made money, fudge, and
   lemon ice.
When I was fourteen, you abandoned me, just up
   and died,

foreclosing on affection, cashiering the unerasable
    you in me.
And I don't know why I am as like you as I am,
or cherish your fading traces as deeply as I do.

## AT THE BORDER OF CONSTANT DISASTER

only the infants
too young to know of tries
can travel to the bottom
and give outrage a name

and answer through sleep
a permanent defiance

only the infants
too pure to know false tenderness
can make the stiff comfort of cardboard
softer than the lava of exile

and anchor through sleep
a permanent defiance

only the infants
too wise to contend with truth
refuse the bread of death and pestilence
refuse the wine of war and famine

and assume through sleep
a permanent defiance

## KAFKA

Kafka, you should have been a black man,
you know, a <u>black</u> black man,
a parable scraping a furnace
for signs of life.
Kafka, you should have been wombed
in Khartoum or Abidjan,
birthed in a dry season,
your iced brilliance blending with the soil.
Kafka, you should have been a native,
you know, a Kaddish-bearer,
a synagogue of suffering.
Kafka, you know,
you should have told Europe you were a Kaffir.

# JAZZ TO JACKSON TO JOHN
### *(for John Reese)*

## movement one: genesis

it must have been something like
sheets of sound wrinkled
with riffs and scats,
the aftermath of a fierce night
breezing through the grits and gravy;
or something like a blind leviathan
squeezing through solid rock,
marking chaos in the water
when his lady of graveyard love went
turning tricks on the ocean's bottom;
or something like a vision
so blazing basic, so gutbucket, so blessed
the lowdown blues flew out: jazz

jazz to Jackson and
dust to dawn and
words for John

it must have been something like
Farish Street in the bebop forties,
a ragtag holy ghost baptizing Mississippi
on an unexpected Sunday, a brilliant revelation
for Billie telling you about these foolish thing

30

back in your own backyard, angel eyes in the rose
    room,
Monk's changing piano into horn because it was
    zero in the sun,
and around midnight there was nobody but you
to walk Parker and his jazz to Jackson;
yeah, brother, it must have been something
striking you like an eargasm,
a baritone ax laid into soprano wood,

like loving madly in hurting silence,
waiting to fingerpop this heathen air
with innovations of classical black
at decibles to wake the deaf, the dumb, and the dead;
because around midnight there was nobody but you
who dug whether race records were
lamentations or lynchings: jazz

jazz to Jackson and
sunset to dawn and
words for John


**movement two: blues people in the corn**

steal away, steal away, steal away
the heart blow/horn blow/drum drop
to bass/five-four time beat

making a one o'clock comeback creep
behind all that jazz
beat — beepbeep — beat
steal way back to beginning
beginning
is the water
is the soul
is the source
is the foundation with my brothers
is Pharaoh jamming in the pyramid,
sketches of Spain for a night in Tunisia;
is MJQ, Tatum, Turrentine, Tyner,
the Jazz Messengers, messiahs, crusading
headhunters tracking down the mind

cause, Lord yes, all God's people got sold
and who'da thought
owning rhythm was a crime like stealing a nickel
and snitching a dime, when we had coffers packed
with golden music and time, golden music and time

sliding from the flesh, the bone, honeysweet music;
them lollipopcicle people
and they sardine ships
(and no music to speak of)
they stole it all and sold it all
for wooden nickels, for frozen dimes: jazz

behind all that jazz
blues people in the corn, in the vale of cotton tears,
blues people in the corn,
waiting, waiting, waiting,
waiting in esoteric patience,
waiting to steal away,
steal away, steal away
soon as Miles runs down the voodoo avenue
with some jazz to Jackson
and pipes a private number
to call a tune for John


**movement three: and this, John, is our new day**


and this, John, is our new day.
never say goodbye to the blues that saw you through,
nor put down the spirituals and the salty
    sermonnettes
the drugs, the junkies, the jukebox juice, the sweat
and the pain of shelling hot peanuts, hot peanuts:
    jazz

and the jazz you gave to us
we give to you as jazz to Jackson and
because we really want to thank you
words for John

# MIDDLES

Complete incompletes

Imperatives conspire

## OPENING NIGHT

schooled in this
theatre of cruelty
you can weather
i believe, i want to believe,
anything falling from the sky,
and i believe i want you to believe
i never left the ground

i believe i want you to believe
this is really real love
not a fable
into which we happened
a romance ago
i believe
(and I know now how you know it)
the chore of love
Is hardly tender
but better yet
rough rolling and rocking
the way of square circles
and waiting inside
yourself for a scene,
an implosion of fire
on fire in fire

i believe I want you to believe
you believe when you go
i'll come into wells of satisfaction
sloshing and grunting
from your throat
and my tongue
tastes passion and electricity
cell by naked cell

i believe i want you to believe
i give your body
a standing ovation
when you stun me
with your opening tight
like lightening
on the ridges of my rod

## SERIOUS

It's as serious
as your life
when smoke gets in your eyes
and a sophisticated lady
lights a fire in your bone
and nothing will be as it was tomorrow
and nothing will be as it was tomorrow
as the magic of passion
lays arsenic and old lust upon your tongue
and the sharps and flats
of reality vanish in the dark
                  in the dark

as she shakes you
up and down
like a pair of dice
and all the liquids
turn from tepid water into steam
and she, so sure and so serene
on the secret dream within your dream

and nothing will be ever
as it was today
with your toes feeling
like the roots of eternity
making love to the dust when you came

and you are elevated
six stories down
with your emotions gone totally astray
in the fastbreak narrative of pillow talk

and you can no longer see
to find the beacon lights of home,
because it's as serious
as your life when a lady lays you out
among her petals and her thorns
and you be howling like a hurricane
with a volcano in your bone
and nothing will be nothing will be
as it was as it was as it was
tomorrow.

## KWANSABA 61907

*(for Richard Wright)*

Ironies abound. Think. Jazz with crazy demons.
Little gods, you call them, little gods.
Study the fine art of coming apart.
Choose now. Chance coils into change. Resent.
Taste truth. Spit it out. Repent. Halt.
Little gods breed. Beyond evil. Beyond good.
Here be blues. Strange. Cold. Forever.

## MOMENT #1: WHEN IT RAINS: MORTON SALT
## POEM FOR QUO VADIS GEX BREAUX

When it rains, we pour
wry libations. We are salt.
When summoned, we testify.
We sprinkle our selves with water
That has holes in it. The spaces left
when it rains. We pour
silence, healing wounds,
work-wrecked backs,
smashed hearts,
trauma-burdened dreams,
paper-split finer skin,
the too-much that comes
when it pours. We are salt.
Post-Katrina when it pours
we sprint around the sun,
morph to rock,
gleam like love.

## A MODEST PLEA

Shakespeare,
Paragon, patron of plagiarists,
When imagination fails,
Old felon, fly down
From heavenly hell,
Bring a mercy
Of rain dry as dust,
A cold awakening
For a brain's slumber.

## AN APRIL OBSERVATION

PHOTOGRAPHS OF FATHER, OF MOTHER,
EVOKE AMBIGUOUS YEARNINGS TO SMOTHER
IN THE FLASH OF AN IDEA: LOVE AS
DIGITAL RECREATION. THE ACT HAS
RELEASED ME, RENTED ME AGAIN
IN A CONTRACT WHERE ACHIEVEMENT'S NEVER
   BEEN.
AS USUAL, THE GAZE EXCEEDS THE FRAME,
INTRUDES LIKE A SEARCHLIGHT IN DEEP FOG,
THE MIST SOFT, TEPID, LIKE WINTRY SLEEP.
I KNOW WELL THIS PLACE I AM, ITS GAME,
ITS RANDOM TRAPS BENEATH THE BOG.
ALL THOSE TINTEDPROMISES WOULD NOT KEEP.
NITRATE ROLLS LIKE WORDED SAND.
AH, STIGMATA, MEMORY IN MY HAND.

## A PEAPICKING PRAYER (1979)

He had rolled
along, a long way
into the black song of poplarville.
He mississippied
bayou country, in a slow hurry
to sip the oil of Ollie street,
to grease his axle on bourbon.
In tumble-weedy texas
tacos and mary jane
mesmerized his lips.

The dry drizzle
of buffalo made him New York
in German to California.
The flow of peaceful vineyards
blessed his brain.

California dreaming.
Its blue persuasion
laid pounds of fever
on his back. Love and a trade wind
blew him east again.
He had trouble shock.

Louisiana healed him. Sometimes.
When he had a show-me state of mind,

he inched north, remembered his grandmother's
    tree,
1946, how to stumble through the divining circle.

When last seen, he was reading
under the light of a crystal stair.

## TRANSITION

We refuse to scrumble
At this hour (or ever)
The discipline of dying.

*You chose, it was your choice*
*To enter the color of pain*
*And rename your bone and skin*
*Dried snowflake for a scattering of desire.*

*You took the daredevil option*
*To reset a clock of disbelief,*
*To make lore with a copacetic muse,*
*To be salt on the floor.*

Few of us have your art.
How hard it must have been
To beat grief at his own game.

## THE BODY POLITIC

Apologize
Your ears

They'll not be long here
Or hearing

Your eyes deny
The mortality of your thumb

Deify
Soon and very soon

Romance your mouth
With democratic taste

Seduce your nose
Gain the strength to climb

## SALVATION

*(for Niyi Osundare)*

Griot, in your mother-tongue, proclaim:
How wet in this world are words.

Married tears in the attic of the August moon
Soon discover "hope"/"help" are
Syllable fluent as sweet bamboo
Flagellating wind: breath blinding memory:
How wet are words in this world.

On the third day of tyranny
Flame trees call your name:
Child of the river, oh-sun-daring man,
Lake and sea, ocean-crossing
Ancestors unborn to protect you:
How are words wet in this world.

Child of the river, once you and I
Were arrogant pronouns
*Wading* a gulf, *warning* a clan
When child-blood diamond soldiers
*Knife, rope and bullet* love, rain *forbids*
Flower-petals *to butterfly* air:
In this world how are words wet.

Intimate losses prepare salvation.
*Felix culpa* never-won day
When sound shall banish transgressions
And conceive us in the womb of speech,
Extracting innocence from guilt
And holiness from levee cane:
Griot, in my mother-tongue, announce:
In this world how wet words are.

## 4&5 REMIX FOR 3&8/BDAY JAZZ FOR DAVE/ THREE HOURS IN 1967

*(for Dave Brinks)*

People poetry
inside the sun

Clarinets inspire crawfish
To jitterbugwaltz
around

the moon and
birthday jazz to bathe in soul — May day, may day,
    any day now

When Blackwell tenderized
A log of rhythm

the magic of juju made
Shepp whisper: "Sorry bout that; hypnosis happens!"

Miles chewed a blue note
Growling: "So what?"

Already there — grooving on a Thursday afternoon,
Liberating a tunnel's vision

**CrickCrescent**

The birth of the cool


**CrackCrescent**

Fermenting a question
encrusted and entrusted
with obsidian diamonds hidden in the heart

Inside the sun
A blind wheelchair
Protested a path

It could not see
But heard it say

"Three, four, eight/let us intimidate, intimidate,
   intimidate."


Spewing fumes of Dixie,
        Dixieland,
                Dixiedizzyworld,
                        Dixie 45,
Look away,
Waterblast and baptize away,

52

Brutalize and segregate the communion altar/ the
    wasteland lynched away,
        tar the feather
        away, polltax and the bishop will confirm
the carmelized bloodline away,
trading sevens and the baker's dozens away:

a lesson before the dying away

confederated dunces dreaming away

our lives lockjawed away: it all went so fast! Giants
    do not bow down.

Already there/here in the way
Tony Williams took
Confusion to fusion,
Unlocking

Yeah you right,
the path
 Miles Davis
Blew along
 on his way
to find
Nefertiti,
 blew hard bop through the stargate
to find

Nefertiti
scanned a Shorter map
 to find...

where—yes, it must mean New Orleans—
4 & 5 remix for 3 & 8
Makes a birthday
The palaver of jazz tongues
Tasting sounds
And loving to live a poetry inside the sun.

## LOVE IN A FOREIGN HOUSE

I have wounded you.


The silence of your grief
Resonates between us

Loud as the screams
Of a dead soldier
Dancing on phantom legs.

Life is tough; love, tougher
In a foreign house.
Pretend to be home.

## POEMS OF GUILT AND INNOCENCE

1) Deposition of an electric chair on the death of
   an innocent man:

### SORRY

2) Thirty days ago

In hot blood the bullets
Dispatched my mistaken identity.

At the trial the lawyer argued
The cop thought I was a life-sized FBI poster

Him the jury found innocent as charged
And me guilty of impersonating an official
   document.

## FRAGILITY

WHERE NOW ARE THEY
WHO CALLED BOB KAUFMAN A FOOL
FOR CHANTING THE ANCIENT RAIN

HUSH, HUSH, THE OIL IS CALLING
YOUR NAME, NAME WHAT SHALL YOU DO
HUSH, BE GLAD, TROUBLEMS DO NOT LAST
ALWAYS, ALL WAYS THE SUN SHINES
AND OIL AIN'T GOT LONG TO BE HERE

WHERE ARE THEY NOW
WHO CALLED BOB KAUFMAN CRAZY
FOR CHARTERING ANCIENT RAIN

## BLOOD AND BLACK FIRES

And this is not a poem

I smell blood and black fire! Blood and black
  fire!
I see/hear an American mother crying. I see a
  father with a sign.

"You took my son away from me! You know how
hard it was for me to get him to stay in school and
graduate? You know how many black men graduate?
Not many!"

Michael Brown's mother wept out, said,
Weeping in the showed-me Missouri
Amorality of the television screen:

"Because you bring them down to this type of level
where they feel they don't got nothing to live for
anyway! (They feel) they gonna try to take me out
anyway!"

Weeping in the showed-me Missouri
Near the mighty Mississippi, Michael Brown's
  mother

Authorized grief to bring her words to thee,
Old put out the sun god, put out the moon god,
Put out the universe god.

And the big animal wearing the badge of authority
    called
All the little animals wearing no authority to be
    angry,
Just rudely, grassrooty nude in the no-clothing of
    angry,
Running and grabbing and shouting ancient sonics —
Out of their minds but in yours—
The big animal called all the little animals
Washed in the blood of the Lamb's confusion

"Anymules. Fucking anymules,"
Using the authority of his authority ,
Justifying, certifying, sanctifying
The sport the god of violence has with men.

Try to write down as many of the signs as you can,
Try to get as many of the people's documents as you
    can.
Slaughter us with remembering this is not a modest
    proposal
In forty-one Baraka verses which are also curses,

This is not a proposal for anybody's death, this is
   not a poem.
This is not a retold how somebody blue/blew up
   American again.

**I smell blood and black fire! Blood and black**
   **fire!**
**I see / hear an American mother crying. A son**
   **dying. I see a father with a sign.**
**I remember since before eternity what the god of**
   **violence ordains.**

**And this is not a poem.**
**This is a eulogy for a dead rainbow.**

LET THE SHIT HIT THE FAN.
I SMELL BLACK FIRE AND BLOOD
AND BLACK BLOOD AND FIRE
AND THE FINALITY THAT IS THE GENESIS.

AND WILL THE FURIOUS FLOWER BLOOM ON
THE GRAVE OF MICHAEL BROWN?

## PREGNANT MEMORIES OF YOUR LIVE-IN BOYFRIEND AND YOUR BABY'S BABY-DADDY: NOTES ON AN EVERYDAY AFFAIR

Precious memories, how they linger,
Linger, linger, run down my finger
Precious memories perverted—
Then they flood her soul

With the fatal stillness of the midnight
Hot festering wet light, locked uptight
Madness growing fonder, as I ponder
My trueblood jones
As I ponder
My blueblood jones
As I ponder
My instant-satisfaction jones
And the pregnant precious scenes unfold.

They bone the screen, spill sperm at the tea party
Because America — she too dumb to know
Where to put her Oscar or her Oedipus
Or find the global balm of warning on the Internet
    of her soul!

Precious memories, how they linger,
Linger, linger, run down my finger
Precious memories perverted —

Then they flood her soul,
Because America — she too dumb to know
Where to put her Oscar or her Oedipus,
To know DUI is not IUD.

When the momma make me holler
And my daughter make me moan
The precious memories ever flood my soul,
Unfolding soft blood diamonds and smoking
    cocaine gold;
When the baby-momma make me scream and holler
And our daughter be truth-paralyzed
In the organic wetness of the midnight,
In the casual rape of her bluest eyes
Movied like Sarah's pitbull lipstick traces on a joint
Movied like the carnal knowledge of her trash talk,
The carnal knowledge of her Eight Mile trailer trash
As I told the baby-momma it sure be good for her.

Precious memories, how they tingle,
Tingle, tingle down my phallic symbol,
Symbol, symbol as you get up to get down
Down low low down into the skin,
Into flesh fresh velvet erotic tragedies.

**Let it blow, let it flow, she ain't got nowhere else
to go. Age ain't nothing but a number.**

*But she was only 16, only 16, precious, virgin in the vile middle
passing......*

**So, so what? I'm a lover. Daddy was.**

*But she was only 16, only 16, precious, brother.
You better wind your clock, brother; brother, you better check your
cock.
Because your ain't right. Can't you recall jellyroll killed your daddy,
drove your momma stone blind?*

**Bullshit, punk! That's how we roll. Your advice
flunked.**

Teen's mom arrested for ignoring rapes, police say,
For accessorizing rapes in the Gucci/Coach
    imitation of her life.

Precious crimes, how they linger
In the race-blind ejaculations of democracy!

A man pleads guilty to rape of 13-year-old
Precious memories.

Man pleads guilty with glee,
His perverted memories lingering
Because law in this Republic can say
The only aggravated rape is the rape of a victim
    younger than 13.

Such memories spun in the swastika of time.

But she was 16 and she screamed and her momma
    wouldn't listen.
So what? It is a man's nature to appropriate the
    pleasure
And precious memories of power, catholic apolo-
    getics for slaves and abused altar boys,
Careless law, oh careless legalized illegal law ——
Seven lively sins linger, linger, linger,
Run down my finger

Precious memories          **(ain't that right, dawg?)**

Precious memories          **(ain't that right, dog?)**

Precious memories and pain linger, linger, linger
In this man's world that is nothing without the
    woman and the girl
Weary, angry and weary, praying for respect, praying
    to God for a love named human rights,

Praying for love that does not come in the stillness
  of the midnight,
Praying for a time when precious, sacred scenes
  indeed unfold.

## THAT DAY THE RAINBOW DIED

*(for people who prey darkly)*

Was not a holy day
In the life eternal
But a cheapening
Of experience in a life,
A first supper of things unknown

Was an experience
Mainly of a drained trope
Coming bereft of faith,
Coming mainly to a dance,
Dangling in a terminal hope

Was an occasion
For an experience,
For the body and the blood,
The wine and the bread
The cigar and the gun
All passing through alembics

Was a transubstantiation
An experience of tragedy
Between your segregated god
And mine, the sacrifice, mock magic,

Severe cannibals communing
In temporary grace
That day the rainbow died.

## ENDS

Complete incompletes

Imperatives conspire

## TRAYVON: YOUR EYES ARE HAUNTING ME

*"Would you wear my eyes?"*
Bob Kaufman

Compassion, would you wear my eyes?
Did you say you'd wear my eyes?
Would you read the gothic tale of life
Leaking from the double helix of my skin?

Compassion, did you see what I saw
When you broke the fifth seal of the watch
So I could see death praying after me?
See what you have done.


Blood-blinding white
Around my invisible race:
America, old negated rainbow
Smeared on the paralyzed sky.

Mercy, would you wear my eyes to see
Crosswires training on my suspicious back?
Mercy, are you drunk with the blood of saints,
Feasting on hate-blessed manna in the gated
   neighborhood?

See what you've undone:
Sprigs of green dying in a sea of glass.
Love, would you wear my eyes?
Did God say you could wear my eyes?

Trayvon, your eyes are haunting me.
Essence of innocence is haunting me.
Afflicted with angers, now I see
The bullets that came for you are coming for me.

Your eyes are haunting me.
They're watching the negated rainbow.
Compassion, mercy and love in your eyes are
    cheapened dust,
And I shall wear your eyes until revelations scream:
    *"what is just?"*.

## HE HAS WONDERFUL EYES

His eyes, flashlights
To brighten ceilings
Of possibility

Wonderful, his eyes are wonderful,
Our lodestars
To another country
Where streets do talk
And carry our names
And carry our evidence
Of things not seen
In our going at dawn to meet the man.

Wonderful, his eyes are wonderful
With visions above our heads.
In the rhythms of our blues
He finds the price of the ticket,
The precise time to tell
How long the train's been gone.
Wonderful, too, the day
He was lost, his writing
Notes to a native son
About dialogues, raps on race,
The strength of contrition.

His eyes, scissors
To destroy silken webs of deceit.

Wonderful, his eyes are wonderful,
Our beacons
On the fire next time,
The flaming leaves of grass,
The human wrecks entangled
In buzzard-painted clouds.

Wonderful, his eyes are wonderful
Lanterns to enlighten
Those who wash their faces
In superstition
Or suck the milk of death.
His eyes, prophets
To proclaim what we shall tell
Upon the mountain when we finally know his name.

## POEM 69

I hate

                    You as you are

I love

                    You as you are

We adore and adorn

                    You as you are

        In tattered blues.

## WINTER SOLITUDE

Funeral follows funeral —
the second line between —
resentment segregates the tombs.

*The universe is wrinkled*
*with the whims and the winds.*
Saints cut of silk, frantic like the turf,
wanting terror to touch down,
explore lucid leaves of grass
 evermore,
for the asking
 is nevermore.
*The universe is wrinkled*
*with the whims of mothball hours.*
Time. An old man erect,
folding the canals of his bones.
An old woman, pious,
rigid in her rapture on an urn,
grinning toothless passion.
*The universe is wrinkled*
*with the whims of worried days.*
Words copulate not
none the less but more.
Salvation burns
where peace be still
is still to be.

*The universe is wrinkled*
*with the whims of stinging seconds.*

Sounds, jazz iced down,
signal the ending
always beginning
time. Sufferings in ascetic hymns
wash. Absolute soap for the soul.
Primate wings renounce a name.
Yes, seeded clichés. Pungent despair
in the fragrant dust. Flowers rust.
Gravity marks wasting time.

## REPARATIONS: a process poem

Repair/rat/ions
        ion(s)/>is on

Re(pai)<(r)<ations    rationales   rat/ion (ale) s
          ↑                          ↓
Repay      c        repay actions = sale/rations
↕         ↓                     ⅗ person

Repair/rat/ion (ale)  s
          ↕
        Railriper(ape)(rope)

Re(rap)ation

       (for us/them
       for them July 4$^{th}$
       for us 4$^{th}$ of July)

Repair/rat/ions
        ion(s)/>is on<(rape)(nations)

/(for us/them
for them July 4<sup>th</sup>
for us 4th of July )/


Re(pai)<(r)<ations     rationales     rat/ion (ale) s


Repair/rat/ions
            ion(s)/>is on,<(rap)))(((nations)

Re(pai)<(r)<ations     rationales     rat/ion (ale) s

Is on

REPARATIONS: a process poem

## UNCLE SAM AND UNCLE TOM

*(for Charlie Braxton and C. Liegh McInnis)*

After Ferguson, Friday
Chokeheld Crusoe;
Occam's razor shaved Sam's face.

The itch barked.
Tom forgot his place.

## FOOTNOTE 666

Law-ordained, ordered arrogance forms
The halos around uniforms, batons, guns,
Badges, handcuffs, and stuff inform
Novenas for freshly minted killers.
*Injustice is all.*
This is the way the resolute signs morph
Into rabid symbols after the oaths in blue
Confirm this fraternity shall ruthlessly signify
Innocents are predestined to die.
*Injustice is all.*
Feral blue uniforms furiously pray
Their prey shall be young, female/male, and black,
Head bowed, silent, hands empty, arms
    outstretched —
In truth, a crucifix without a cross.
*Injustice is all.*
This is America, after all, and air is a snarky,
    bleached privilege.
Breath of color whose crime is breathing warrants
    social death.
This is America, the new post-Eden, and all blue-
    bloody uniforms know
Justice is a brazen nuisance, a dangerous God-
    fearing whore.

## ~POSTSCRIPT~

### The Doctor Is In

The man is a striking poet hammering syllables and sounds into graceful lyrics and odes. He details our starlight heights as well as assays the depths of our troubled existence. Fractals, the use of recursive geometric patterns, signifies that he is not content with the anecdote or individual achievement, he seeks the truly universal—he wants to understand the cycles of life and the import and impact of collective activity.

Like all humans Ward is both body and soul, flesh and spirit. He understands that any successful effort to fully analyze one aspect, necessarily means considering the other because the measure of humanity is found in the synchronicity of the material and the spiritual. Moreover, the strength of his insights is based on locating the importance of the specific individual within the overall social context. Regardless of achievements, Ward is not overly impressed by any one individual or element considered apart from the social context.

When he writes, Ward's ink is the blood of ancestors and his words are reflections of and on his contemporaries. Make no mistake, however, his vision is of the future. He is concerned about what we make of whom we have been, concerned about what we will do with whatever we have, whatever we have amassed. He knows the past, understands the present, but is mostly dedicated to helping us all deal with the future as both objects shaped by the weight of our environment but also as agents who participate in making the world within which we are born, live and die.

Moreover, Jerry Ward is not an ethnic narcissistic interested only in one particular slice of humanity. Although he has clearly dedicated his life to improving the lot of his people, like his interests in the seemingly divergent areas of science and literature, he throws open his arms to embrace both the history and future of all of us present today on our troubled planet. Thus, there is no contradiction in his deep interest in China that includes yearly, extended stints teaching and lecturing on the other side of the world.

This collection has all the hallmarks of Ward's lifetime of learning and teaching. These poems are songs, or perhaps even psalms. Melding literary allusions, as

disparate as Kaufman and Kafka, profound medita-
tions that merge downhome references with arcane
reflections. The range of his concerns is stupendous:
Shakespeare to Mississippi; jail cell to endowed aca-
demic chair; academic philosophical musings to spot-
on interpretations of contemporary barbershop
bullshit. Like the best of the ancients, no idea, no
place is foreign to him. He has seen more than most
and is conversant with situations and experiences that
are generally considered either rare or strange.
Thankfully, although erudite far beyond average in-
telligence, he possesses an unpretentious personality
that enables him to commune with all levels of society
from street sweeper to college president.

Some are surprised by the surface simplicity of Ward's
poetry. The short pithy lines; the colloquial vernac-
ular peppered with Wilde-like sagaciously selected
bon mots and witticisms; and the startling juxtaposi-
tions of broad philosophical concepts with topical so-
cial manifestations. This is work, like the Bible, full
of amazing phrases crafted with both euphony and
meaning—a handful of examples:

"Audit the maze your flesh has made."

"the underwear of reality"

"sheets of sound wrinkled / with riffs and scats"

"when a lady lays you out / among her petals and her
   thorns"

"When Blackwell tenderized / A log of rhythm"

Over and over we find phrases that delight us in how
he has jammed on words each of which we knew in
their own specificity but whose linkage we never sus-
pected. Consider this tercet:

> "Fermenting a question
> encrusted and entrusted
> with obsidian diamonds hidden in the heart"

What we have here is a poet who dances with angels
and/or jazz masters. When you say his words out loud
you hear the syllabled beats of a rhythm master. Far
too few contemporary poets are as profound in their
use of sound as is this DC-born, Mississippi educated
(in both the formal and informal sense of receiving
an education), New Orleans-based wordsmith. Any
of us can hit a lick once or twice, but to fractal the po-
etic, to weave and re-weave, and weave again a poetic

pattern of words, and to do so with economy, with sense and sensibility (as it were), well, dear reader, that is indeed, a special music worthy of dance as in a secondline celebration.


—Kalamu ya Salaam
July 2015

## FUSION

communed us green
with Guinness and black
from espresso. The snap
of conversation
polished us bright
as boots.

We made us
wiser than
words made us hear
the aching universe,
made us see
eternity's debate
of rifle butts
with bones.
We made us
mankind song

And, yes, we'd sing
again, again.
We'd chant Zimbabwe
so pure
the lasses of Aughrim
could cornrow
their souls.

There's holiness
in speech, in song.

I'd say, a sanctity
the unsuffered
must never touch.

## ABOUT THE AUTHOR

Jerry Washington Ward, Jr., born July 31, 1943 in Washington, D.C., is a retired professor of English and a literary critic who lives in New Orleans, Louisiana. He is the author of *The Katrina Papers: A Journal of Trauma and Recovery* (2008) and *The China Lectures: African American Literary and Critical Issues* (2014).

# TITLES FROM BLACK WIDOW PRESS
## TRANSLATION SERIES

*A Life of Poems, Poems of a Life* by Anna de Noailles. Translated by Norman R. Shapiro. Introduction by Catherine Perry.

*Approximate Man and Other Writings* by Tristan Tzara. Translated and edited by Mary Ann Caws.

*Art Poétique* by Guillevic. Translated by Maureen Smith.

*The Big Game* by Benjamin Péret. Translated with an introduction by Marilyn Kallet.

*Boris Vian Invents Boris Vian: A Boris Vian Reader.* Edited and translated by Julia Older.

*Capital of Pain* by Paul Eluard. Translated by Mary Ann Caws, Patricia Terry, and Nancy Kline.

*Chanson Dada: Selected Poems* by Tristan Tzara. Translated with an introduction and essay by Lee Harwood.

*Creole Echoes: The Francophone Poetry of Nineteenth-Century Louisiana.* Translated by Norman R. Shapiro. Introduction and notes by M. Lynn Weiss.

*Essential Poems and Writings of Joyce Mansour: A Bilingual Anthology.* Translated with an introduction by Serge Gavronsky.

*Essential Poems and Prose of Jules Laforgue.* Translated and edited by Patricia Terry.

*Essential Poems and Writings of Robert Desnos: A Bilingual Anthology.* Edited with an introduction and essay by Mary Ann Caws.

*EyeSeas (Les Ziaux)* by Raymond Queneau. Translated with an introduction by Daniela Hurezanu and Stephen Kessler.

*Fables in a Modern Key* by Pierre Coran. Edited and translated by Norman R. Shapiro. Full-color illustrations by Olga Pastuchiv.

*Forbidden Pleasures: New Selected Poems 1924–1949* by Luis Cernuda. Translated by Stephen Kessler.

*Furor and Mystery & Other Writings* by René Char. Edited and translated by Mary Ann Caws and Nancy Kline.

*The Gentle Genius of Cécile Périn: Selected Poems (1906–1956).* Edited and translated by Norman R. Shapiro.

*Guarding the Air: Selected Poems of Gunnar Harding.* Translated and edited by Roger Greenwald.

*The Inventor of Love & Other Writings* by Gherasim Luca. Translated by Julian & Laura Semilian. Introduction by Andrei Codrescu. Essay by Petre Răileanu.

*Jules Supervielle: Selected Prose and Poetry.* Translated by Nancy Kline and Patricia Terry.

*La Fontaine's Bawdy* by Jean de La Fontaine. Translated with an introduction by Norman R. Shapiro.

*Last Love Poems of Paul Eluard.* Translated with an introduction by Marilyn Kallet.

*Love, Poetry (L'amour la poésie)* by Paul Eluard. Translated with an essay by Stuart Kendall.

*Pierre Reverdy: Poems, Early to Late.* Translated by Mary Ann Caws and Patricia Terry.

*Poems of André Breton: A Bilingual Anthology.* Translated with essays by Jean-Pierre Cauvin and Mary Ann Caws.

*Poems of A. O. Barnabooth* by Valery Larbaud. Translated by Ron Padgett and Bill Zavatsky.

*Poems of Consummation* by Vicente Aleixandre. Translated by Stephen Kessler.

*Préversities: A Jacques Prévert Sampler.* Translated and edited by Norman R. Shapiro.

*The Sea and Other Poems* by Guillevic. Translated by Patricia Terry. Introduction by Monique Chefdor.

*To Speak, to Tell You? Poems* by Sabine Sicaud. Translated by Norman R. Shapiro. Intro-duction and notes by Odile Ayral-Clause.

### Forthcoming Translations

*Earthlight (Clair de Terre)* by André Breton. Translated by Bill Zavatsky and Zack Rogrow. (New and revised edition.)

## MODERN POETRY SERIES

*ABC of Translation* by Willis Barnstone

*An Alchemist with One Eye on Fire* by Clayton Eshleman

*An American Unconscious* by Mebane Robertson

*Anticline* by Clayton Eshleman

*Archaic Design* by Clayton Eshleman

*Backscatter: New and Selected Poems* by John Olson

*Barzakh (Poems 2000–2012)* by Pierre Joris

*The Caveat Onus* by Dave Brinks

*City Without People: The Katrina Poems* by Niyi Osundare

*Clayton Eshleman/The Essential Poetry: 1960–2015*

*Concealments and Caprichos* by Jerome Rothenberg

*Crusader –Woman* by Ruxandra Cesereanu. Translated by Adam J. Sorkin. Introduction by Andrei Codrescu.

*Curdled Skulls: Poems of Bernard Bador.* Translated by Bernard Bador with Clayton Eshleman.

*Disenchanted City (La ville désenchantée)* by Chantal Bizzini. Translated by J. Bradford Anderson, Darren Jackson, and Marilyn Kallet.

*Endure: Poems* by Bei Dao. Translated by Clayton Eshleman and Lucas Klein.

*Exile Is My Trade: A Habib Tengour Reader.* Translated by Pierre Joris.

*Eye of Witness: A Jerome Rothenberg Reader.* Edited with commentaries by Heriberto Yepez & Jerome Rothenberg.

*Fire Exit* by Robert Kelly

*Forgiven Submarine* by Ruxandra Cesereanu and Andrei Codrescu

*Fractal Song* by Jerry W. Ward, Jr.

*from stone this running* by Heller Levinson

*Grindstone of Rapport: A Clayton Eshleman Reader*

*The Hexagon* by Robert Kelly

*Larynx Galaxy* by John Olson

*The Love That Moves Me* by Marilyn Kallet

*Memory Wing* by Bill Lavender

*Packing Light: New and Selected Poems* by Marilyn Kallet

*The Present Tense of the World: Poems 2000–2009* by Amina Saïd. Translated with an introduction by Marilyn Hacker.

*The Price of Experience* by Clayton Eshleman

*The Secret Brain: Selected Poems 1995–2012* by Dave Brinks

*Signal from Draco: New and Selected Poems* by Mebane Robertson

*Soraya (Sonnets)* by Anis Shivani

*Wrack Lariat* by Heller Levinson

**Forthcoming Modern Poetry Titles**

*Dada Budapest* by John Olson

*Fables of Town & Country* by Pierre Coran. Translated by Norman R. Shapiro.

*Funny Way of Staying Alive* by Willis Barnstone

*Geometry of Sound* by Dave Brinks

*Memory* by Bernadette Mayer

*Penetralia* by Clayton Eshleman

## LITERARY THEORY / BIOGRAPHY SERIES

*Barbaric Vast & Wild: A Gathering of Outside and Subterranean Poetry (Poems for the Millennium,* vol. 5). Eds: Jerome Rothenberg and John Bloomberg-Rissman

*Clayton Eshleman: The Whole Art* by Stuart Kendall

*Revolution of the Mind: The Life of André Breton* by Mark Polizzotti

WWW.BLACKWIDOWPRESS.COM